T0039914

# THE BEATLES FOR BANJO

Arranged by Fred Sokolow

with editorial assistance by Ronny Schiff

thanks to Max Calne

ISBN 978-1-4234-5653-7

HAL•LEONARD®
CORPORATION
7777 W. BLUEMOUND RD. P.O. BOX 13819 MILWAUKEE, WI 53213

Copyright © 2009 by HAL LEONARD CORPORATION
International Copyright Secured  All Rights Reserved

For all works contained herein:
Unauthorized copying, arranging, adapting, recording, Internet posting, public performance,
or other distribution of the printed music in this publication is an infringement of copyright.
Infringers are liable under the law.

Visit Hal Leonard Online at
**www.halleonard.com**

# CONTENTS

# And I Love Her

### Words and Music by John Lennon and Paul McCartney

Copyright © 1964 Sony/ATV Music Publishing LLC
Copyright Renewed
This arrangement Copyright © 2009 Sony/ATV Music Publishing LLC
All Rights Administered by Sony/ATV Music Publishing LLC, 8 Music Square West, Nashville, TN 37203
International Copyright Secured   All Rights Reserved

my love,___ you'd love her too._____ I___ love___
- er brings,___ she brings to me,_____ and I love___

***To Coda*** ⊕ **Bridge**

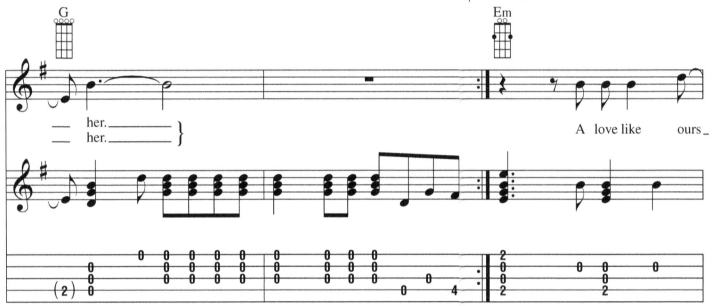

___ her._____ } A love like ours___
___ her._____

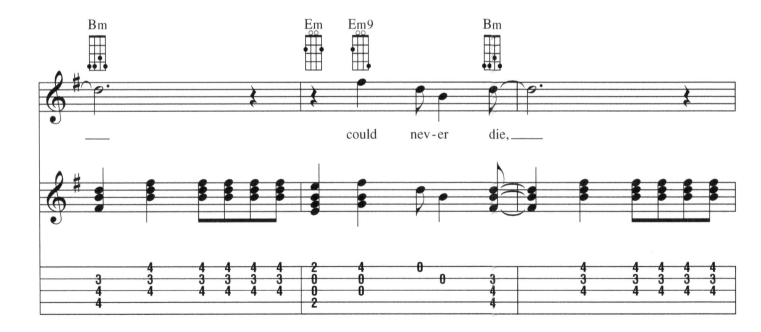

___ could nev-er die,_____

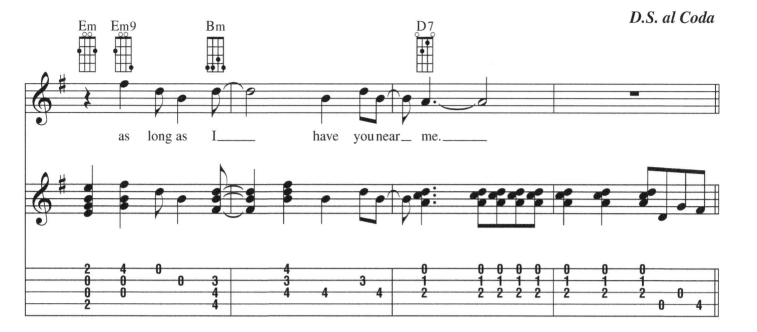

as long as I＿＿＿ have you near＿ me.＿

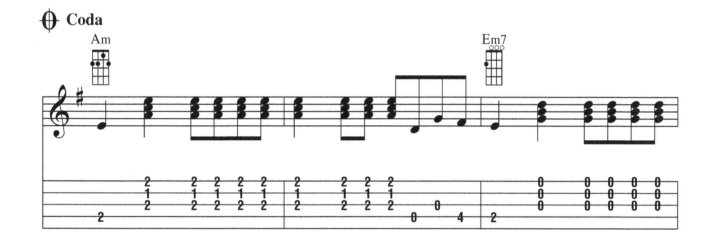

**Coda**

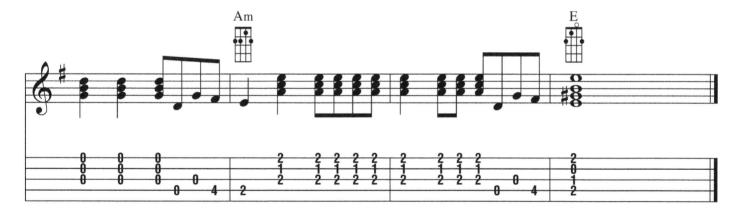

*Additional Lyrics*

3. Bright are the stars that shine, dark is the sky.
   I know this love of mine will never die,
   And I love her.

# Across the Universe

### Words and Music by John Lennon and Paul McCartney

Copyright © 1968, 1970 Sony/ATV Music Publishing LLC
Copyright Renewed
This arrangement Copyright © 2009 Sony/ATV Music Publishing LLC
All Rights Administered by Sony/ATV Music Publishing LLC, 8 Music Square West, Nashville, TN 37203
International Copyright Secured   All Rights Reserved

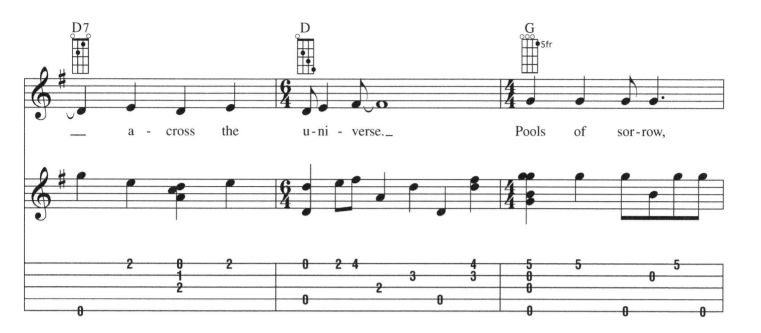

a - cross the u - ni - verse._ Pools of sor - row,

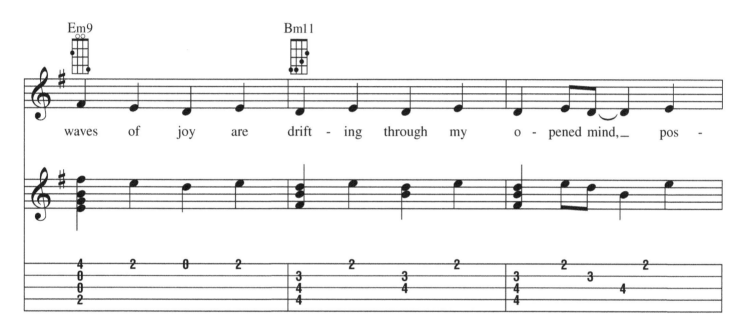

waves of joy are drift - ing through my o - pened mind,_ pos -

sess - ing and ca - ress - ing me._

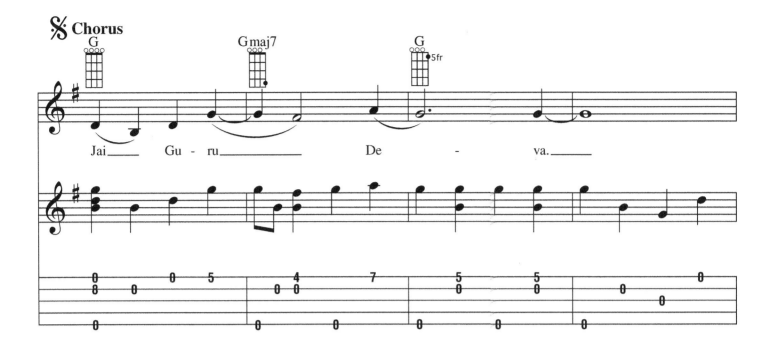

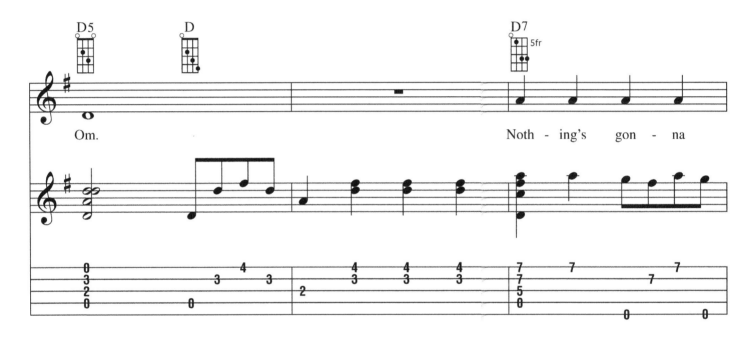

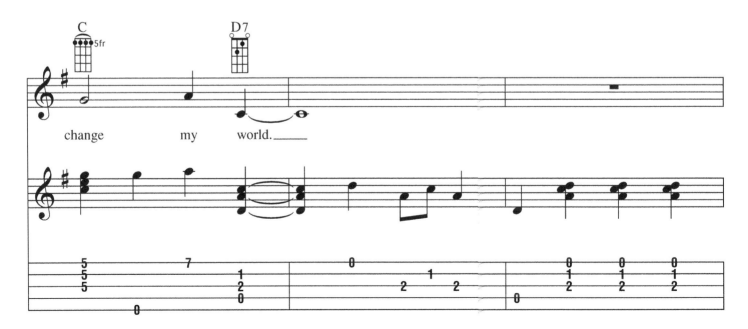

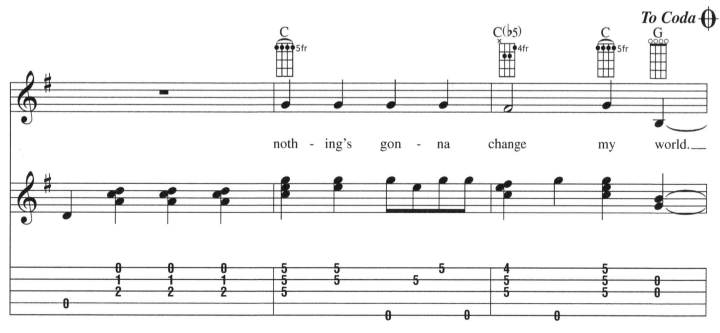

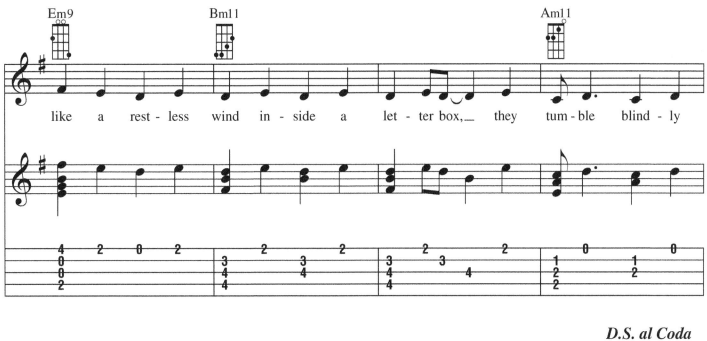

like a rest - less wind in - side a let - ter box,__ they tum - ble blind - ly

*D.S. al Coda*

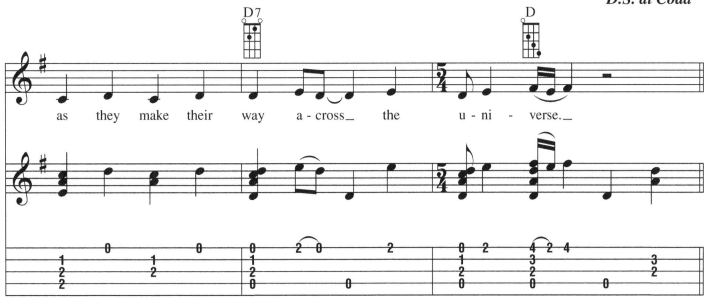

as they make their way a - cross__ the u - ni - verse.__

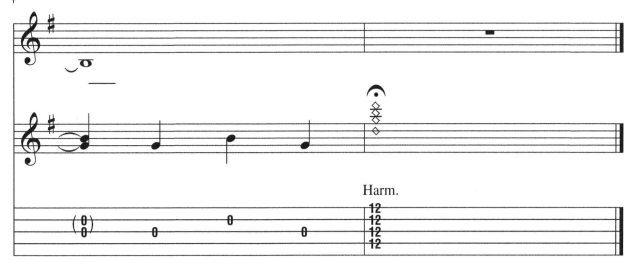

**Coda**

Harm.

# Blackbird

**Words and Music by John Lennon and Paul McCartney**

\* Arranged for basic strum or clawhammer style; index finger picks melody notes.

1., 2. Black - bird sing-ing in the dead of night,

{ take these bro-ken wings_____ and learn to fly. }
{ take these sunk-en eyes_____ and learn to see. }

Copyright © 1968, 1969 Sony/ATV Music Publishing LLC
Copyright Renewed
This arrangement Copyright © 2009 Sony/ATV Music Publishing LLC
All Rights Administered by Sony/ATV Music Publishing LLC, 8 Music Square West, Nashville, TN 37203
International Copyright Secured   All Rights Reserved

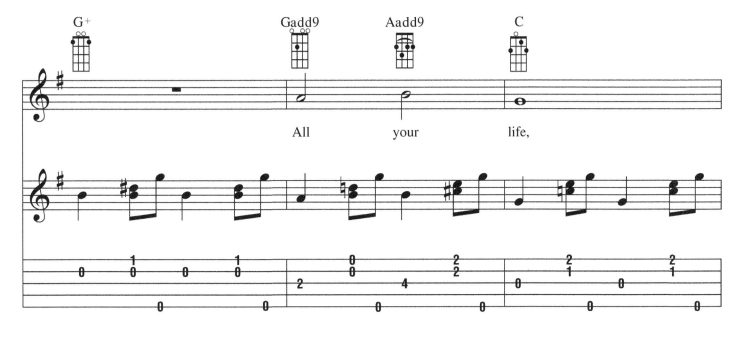

All your life,

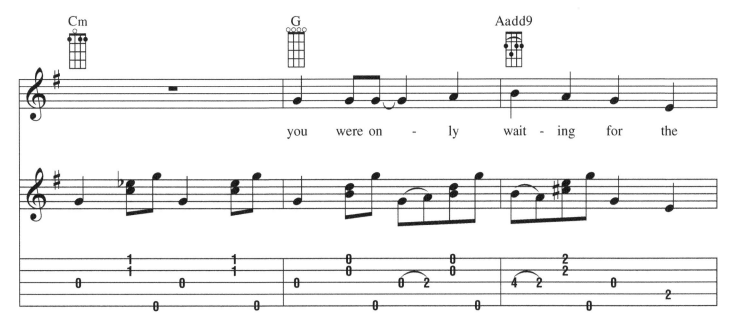

you were on - ly wait - ing for the

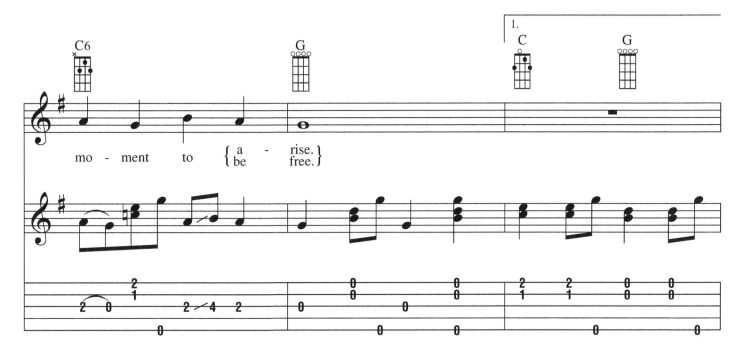

mo - ment to { a - rise. } { be free. }

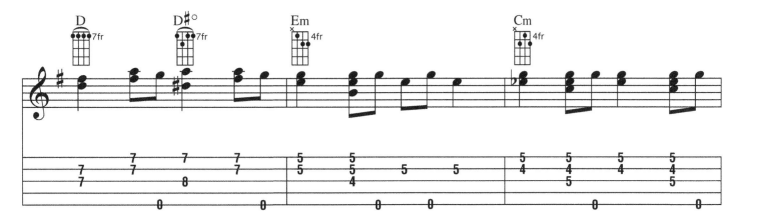

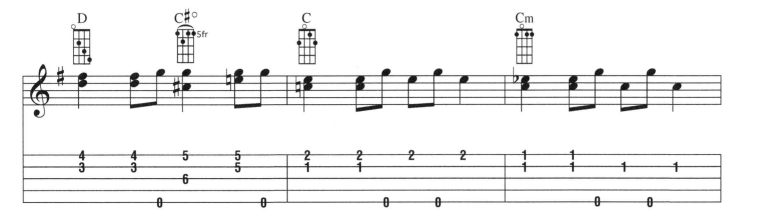

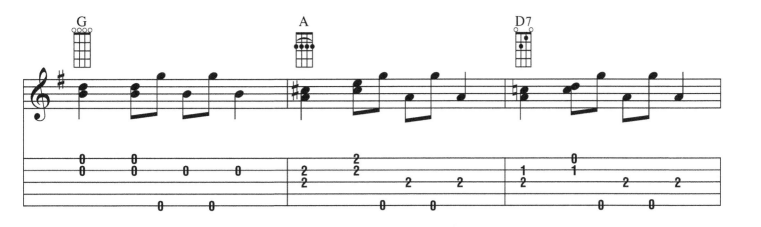

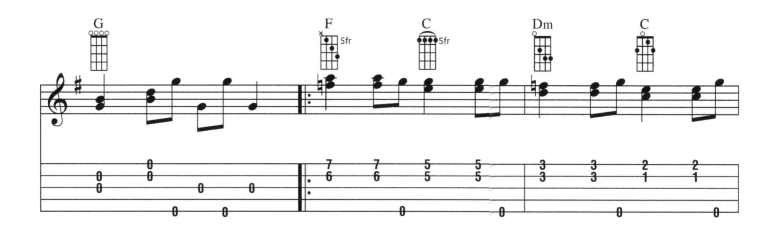

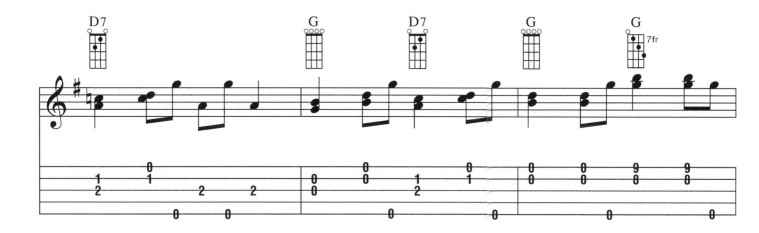

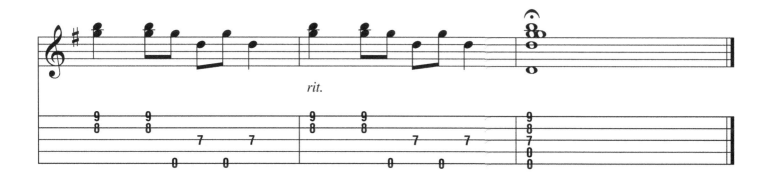

# A Hard Day's Night

**Words and Music by John Lennon and Paul McCartney**

Copyright © 1964 Sony/ATV Music Publishing LLC
Copyright Renewed
This arrangement Copyright © 2009 Sony/ATV Music Publishing LLC
All Rights Administered by Sony/ATV Music Publishing LLC, 8 Music Square West, Nashville, TN 37203
International Copyright Secured   All Rights Reserved

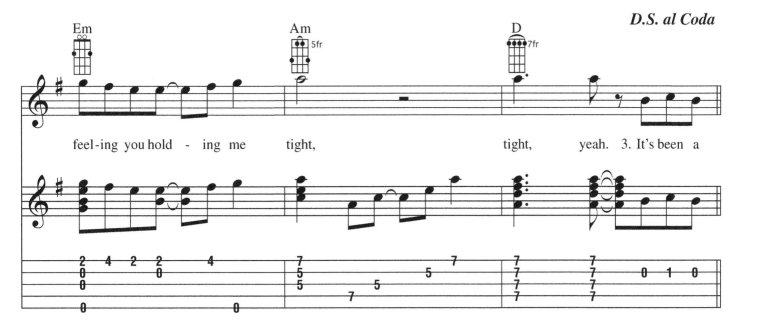

feel-ing you hold - ing me tight,      tight,      yeah. 3. It's been a

**Coda**

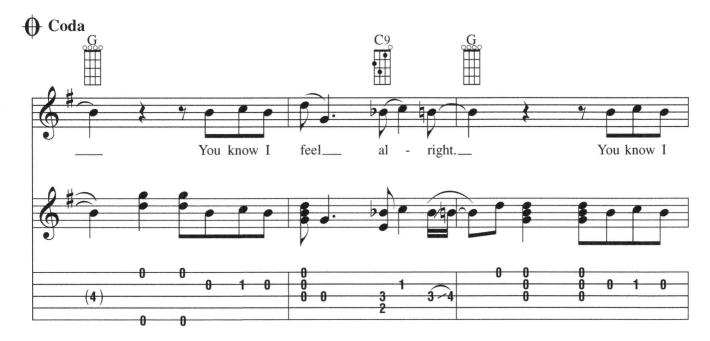

You know I    feel___    al - right.___      You know I

feel      al - right.

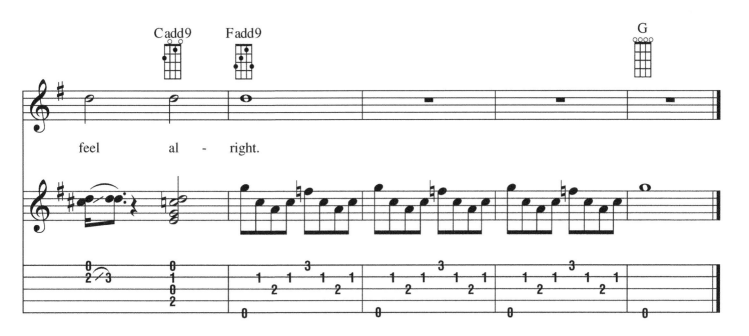

# Eight Days a Week

**Words and Music by John Lennon and Paul McCartney**

Copyright © 1964 Sony/ATV Music Publishing LLC
Copyright Renewed
This arrangement Copyright © 2009 Sony/ATV Music Publishing LLC
All Rights Administered by Sony/ATV Music Publishing LLC, 8 Music Square West, Nashville, TN 37203
International Copyright Secured   All Rights Reserved

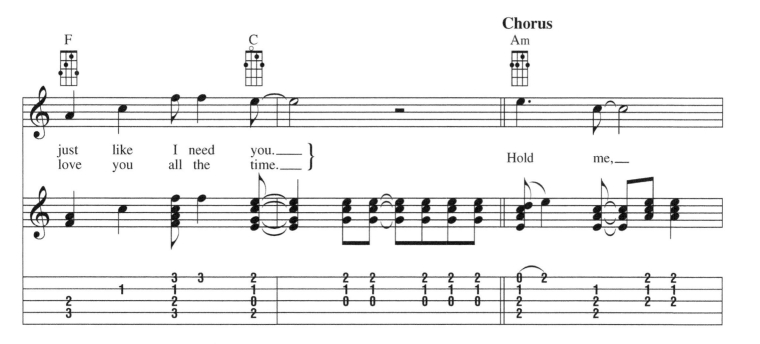

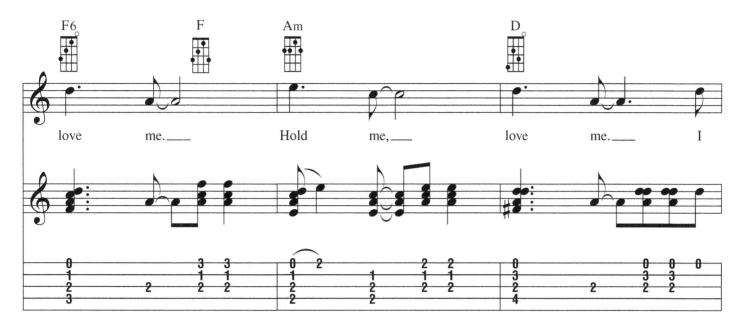

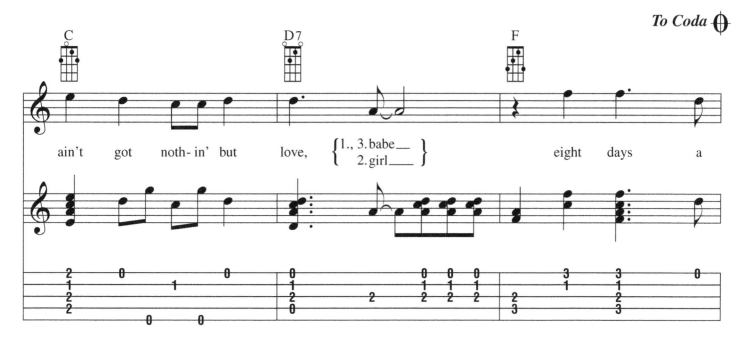

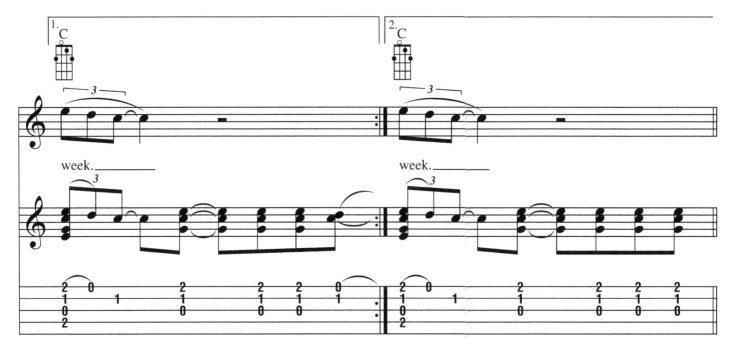

**Bridge**

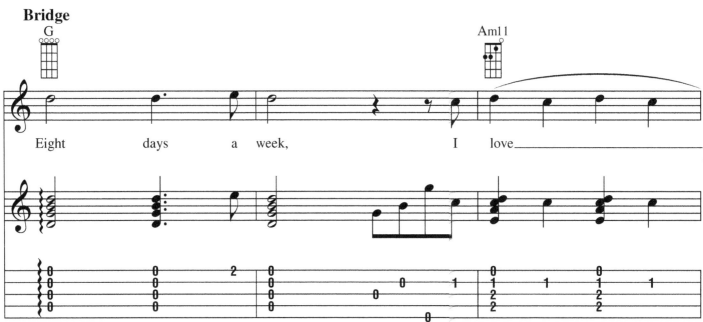

Eight days a week, I love you.

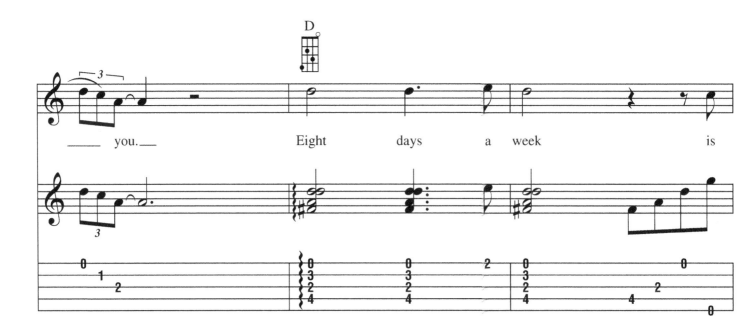

you. Eight days a week is

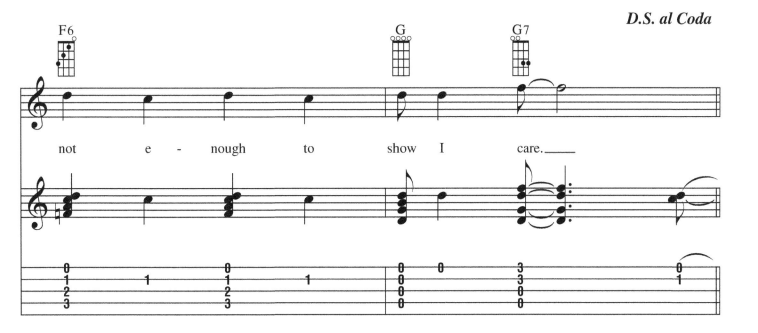

not e - nough to show I care.____

## ⊕ Coda

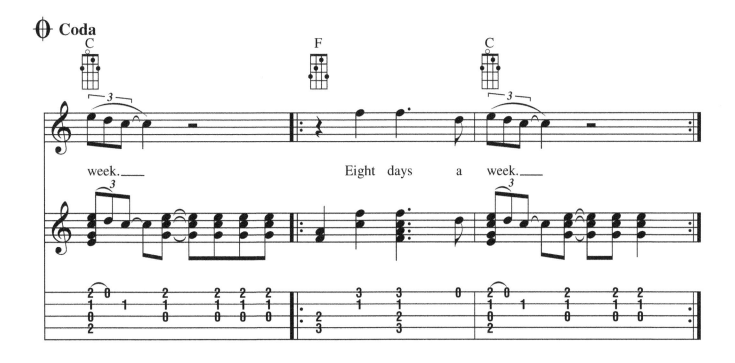

week.____ Eight days a week.____

## Outro

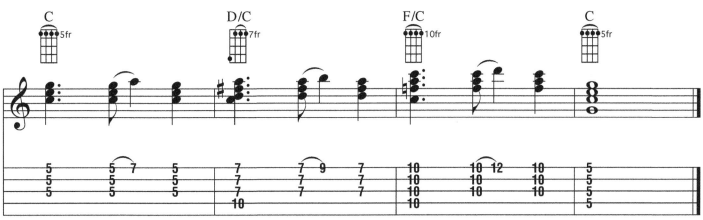

# Here Comes the Sun

**Words and Music by George Harrison**

Copyright © 1969 Harrisongs Ltd.
Copyright Renewed 1998
This arrangement Copyright © 2009 Harrisongs Ltd.
All Rights Reserved

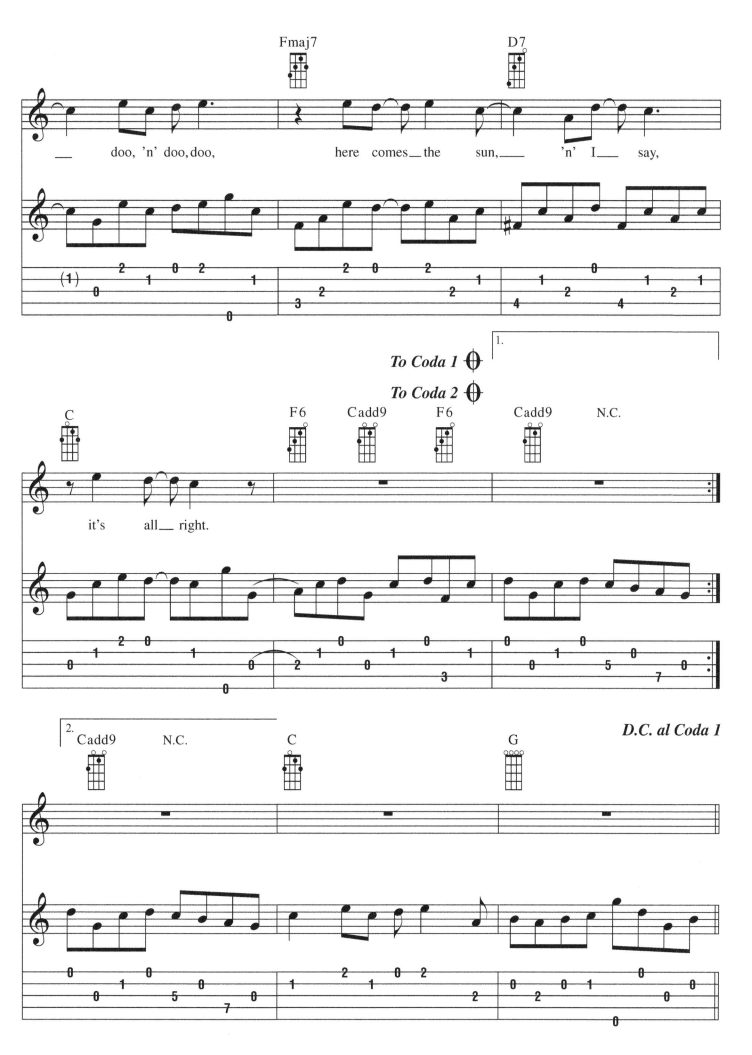

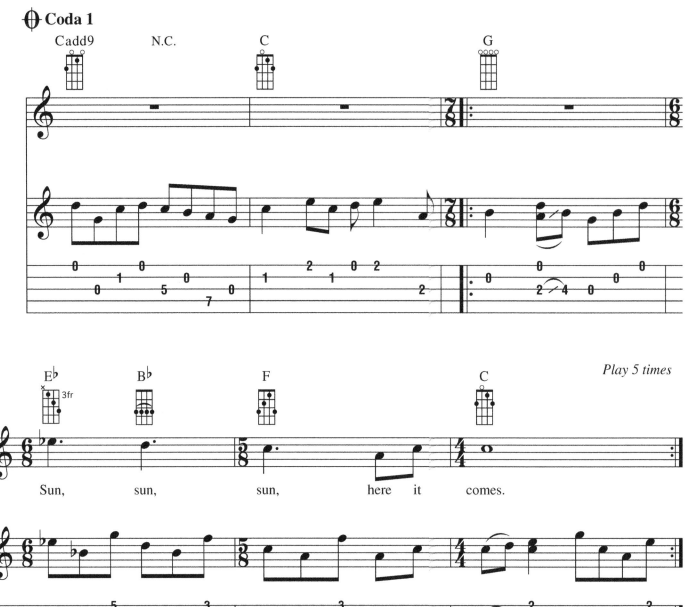

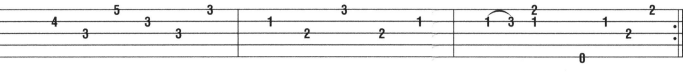

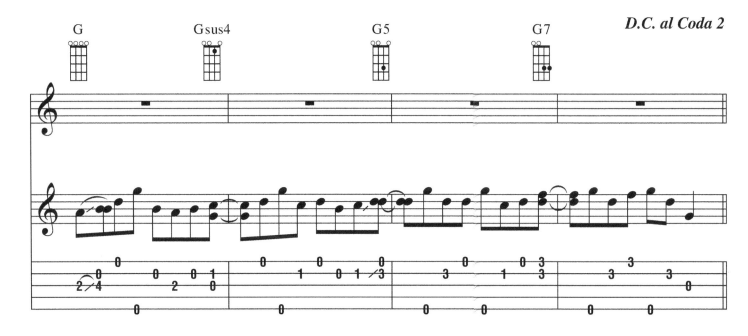

## ⊕ Coda 2

*Additional Lyrics*

3. Little darling,
   The smile's returning to their faces;
   Little darling,
   It seems like years since it's been here.

4. Little darling,
   I feel that ice is slowly melting;
   Little darling,
   It seems like years since it's been clear.

# Hey Jude

**Words and Music by John Lennon and Paul McCartney**

Copyright © 1968 Sony/ATV Music Publishing LLC
Copyright Renewed
This arrangement Copyright © 2009 Sony/ATV Music Publishing LLC
All Rights Administered by Sony/ATV Music Publishing LLC, 8 Music Square West, Nashville, TN 37203
International Copyright Secured   All Rights Reserved

**Bridge**

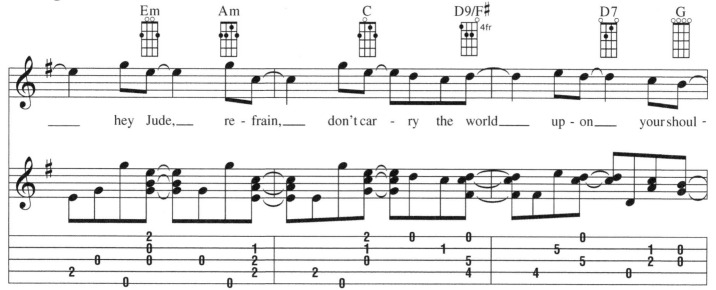

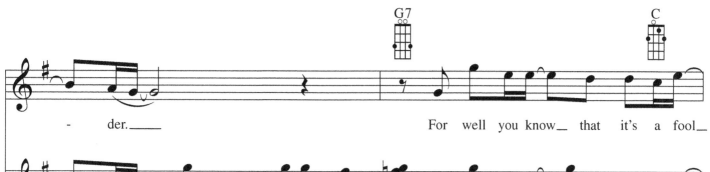

## Outro

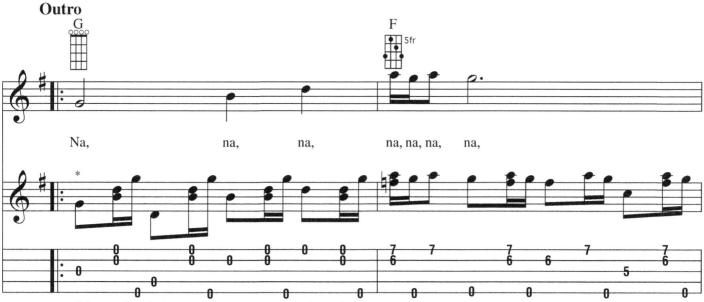

Na, na, na, na, na, na, na,

\* Arranged for basic strum or clawhammer style; index finger picks melody notes.

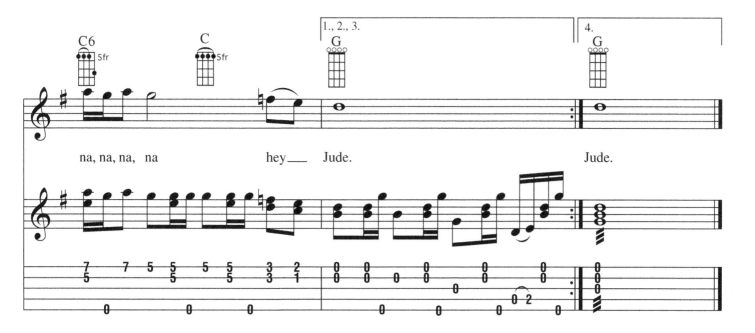

na, na, na, na     hey___ Jude.     Jude.

*Additional Lyrics*

3. Hey Jude, don't let me down.
   You have found her,
   Now go and get her.
   Remember to let her into your heart,
   Then you can start to make it better.

*Bridge:* So let it out and let it in,
   Hey Jude, begin,
   You're waiting for someone to perform with.
   And don't you know that it's just you
   Hey Jude you'll do
   The movement you need is on your shoulder.
   Na, na, na, na, na, na, na, na, na.

4. Hey Jude, don't make it bad,
   Take a sad song and make it better.
   Remember to let her under your skin,
   Then you begin to make it
   Better, better, better, better, better, better, oh!

# In My Life

**Words and Music by John Lennon and Paul McCartney**

Copyright © 1965 Sony/ATV Music Publishing LLC
Copyright Renewed
This arrangement Copyright © 2009 Sony/ATV Music Publishing LLC
All Rights Administered by Sony/ATV Music Publishing LLC, 8 Music Square West, Nashville, TN 37203
International Copyright Secured   All Rights Reserved

bet - ter.    Some have    gone_____    and    some  re - main._    All these

mean - ing    when I    think    of_ love    as    some - thing new.__    Though I

### Chorus

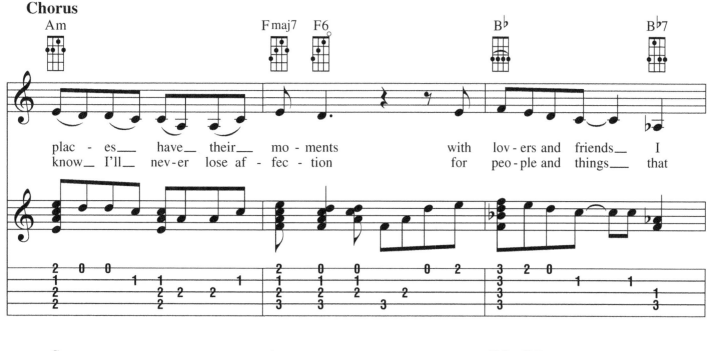

plac - es__  have__  their__  mo - ments    with    lov - ers and  friends__    I

know__  I'll__  nev - er  lose af - fec - tion    for    peo - ple and  things___  that

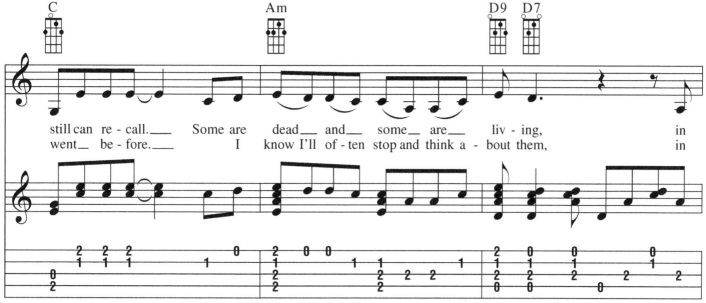

still can re - call.___    Some are    dead__ and__  some_ are__  liv - ing,    in

went_ be - fore.___    I    know I'll of - ten stop and think a - bout them,    in

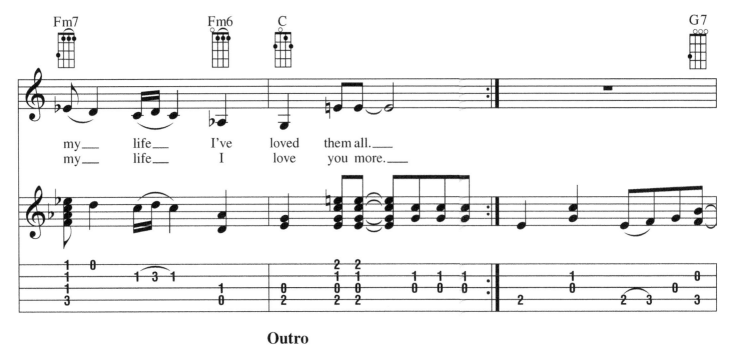

**Outro**

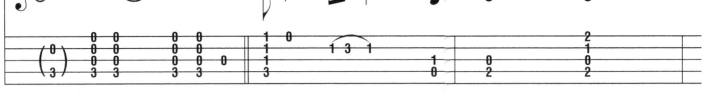

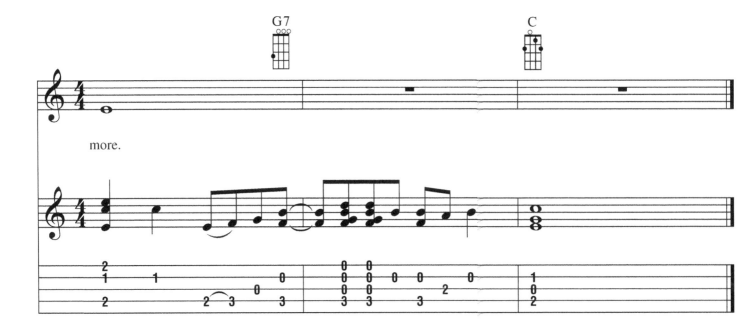

# Lucy in the Sky with Diamonds

**Words and Music by John Lennon and Paul McCartney**

Copyright © 1967 Sony/ATV Music Publishing LLC
Copyright Renewed
This arrangement Copyright © 2009 Sony/ATV Music Publishing LLC
All Rights Administered by Sony/ATV Music Publishing LLC, 8 Music Square West, Nashville, TN 37203
International Copyright Secured   All Rights Reserved

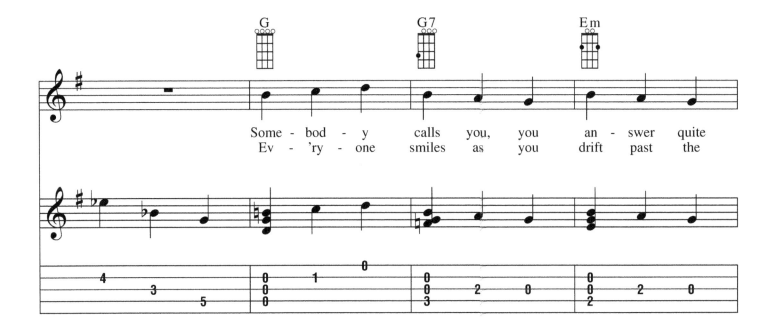

Some - bod - y    calls you,    you    an - swer quite
Ev - 'ry - one    smiles as    you    drift past the

slow - ly,        a    girl    with    ka - lei - do - scope    eyes._____
flow - ers    that    grow    so    in - cred - i - bly    high._____

*To Coda* ⊕
E♭6

**Pre-Chorus**
A♭

Cel - lo - phane
News - pa - per

flow - ers    of    yel - low    and    green
tax - is    ap - pear    on    the    green    shore,

tow - er - ing
wait - ing    to

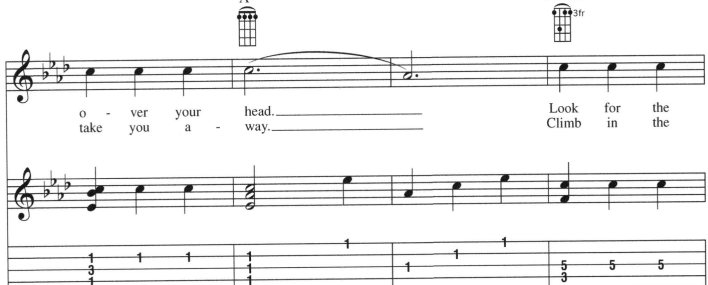

o - ver    your    head._____
take    you    a - way._____

Look    for    the
Climb    in    the

girl    with    the    sun    in    her    eyes    and    she's    gone. }
back    with    your    sun    head    in    the    clouds    and    you're    gone. }

### Additional Lyrics

3. Picture yourself on a train in a station,
   With plasticene porters with looking-glass ties.
   Suddenly someone is there at the turnstile,
   The girl with kaleidoscope eyes.

# Let It Be

**Words and Music by John Lennon and Paul McCartney**

1. When I

*find my-self_ in times of trou-ble, Moth-er Mar - y comes to me,_*
2. *when the bro - ken - heart - ed peo - ple liv - ing in_ the world a - gree,_*
3. *See additional lyrics*

Copyright © 1970 Sony/ATV Music Publishing LLC
Copyright Renewed
This arrangement Copyright © 2009 Sony/ATV Music Publishing LLC
All Rights Administered by Sony/ATV Music Publishing LLC, 8 Music Square West, Nashville, TN 37203
International Copyright Secured   All Rights Reserved

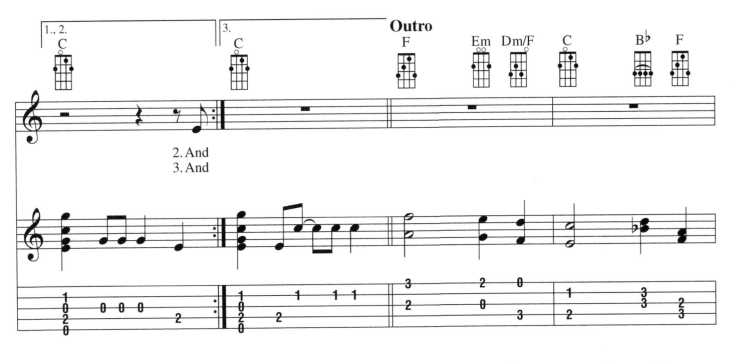

2. And
3. And

*Additional Lyrics*

3. And when the night is cloudy,
   There is still a light that shines on me,
   Shine until tomorrow, let it be.
   I wake up to the sound of music,
   Mother Mary comes to me,
   Speaking words of wisdom, let it be.

# Norwegian Wood (This Bird Has Flown)

**Words and Music by John Lennon and Paul McCartney**

* Arranged for basic strum or clawhammer style; index finger picks melody notes.

Copyright © 1965 Sony/ATV Music Publishing LLC
Copyright Renewed
This arrangement Copyright © 2009 Sony/ATV Music Publishing LLC
All Rights Administered by Sony/ATV Music Publishing LLC, 8 Music Square West, Nashville, TN 37203
International Copyright Secured   All Rights Reserved

good ... Nor - we - gian wood? ... She

## 𝄌 Bridge

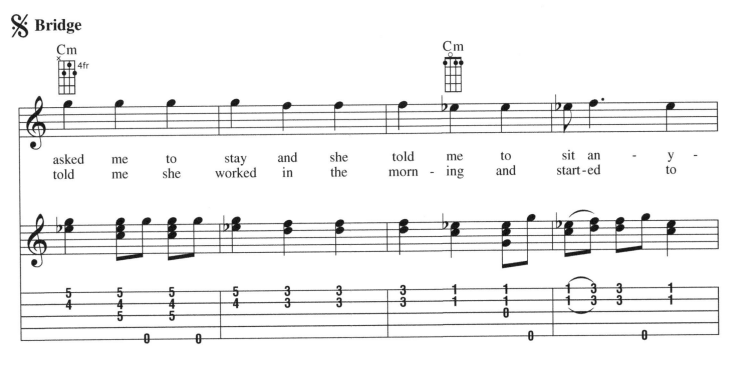

asked me to stay and she told me to sit an - y - where.
told me she worked in the morn - ing and start-ed to laugh.

where. ... So
laugh. ... I

**Outro**

# Please Please Me

**Words and Music by John Lennon and Paul McCartney**

Copyright © 1962, 1964 UNIVERSAL/DICK JAMES MUSIC LTD.
Copyright Renewed and Assigned to UNIVERSAL/DICK JAMES MUSIC LTD., JULIAN LENNON, SEAN ONO LENNON and YOKO ONO LENNON
This arrangement Copyright © 2009 UNIVERSAL/DICK JAMES MUSIC LTD., JULIAN LENNON, SEAN ONO LENNON and YOKO ONO LENNON
All Rights for UNIVERSAL/DICK JAMES MUSIC LTD. in the U.S. and Canada Administered by UNIVERSAL - SONGS OF POLYGRAM INTERNATIONAL, INC.
All Rights Reserved   Used by Permission

# She Loves You

**Words and Music by John Lennon and Paul McCartney**

**Intro-Chorus**
**Bright Rock Beat** ♩ = 158

She loves you, yeah, yeah, yeah.__ She loves you, yeah, yeah, yeah.__ She loves you, yeah, yeah, yeah, yeah.

**Verse**

N.C.      G      Em7      Bm

1. You think you've lost your love,__ well, I saw her yes-ter-
2. She said you hurt her so,__ she al-most lost her
3. *See additional lyrics*

Copyright © 1963 by NORTHERN SONGS LIMITED
Copyright Renewed
This arrangement Copyright © 2009 by NORTHERN SONGS LIMITED
All rights for the U.S.A., its territories and possessions and Canada assigned to and controlled by GIL MUSIC CORP., 1650 Broadway, New York, NY 10019
International Copyright Secured   All Rights Reserved

**Outro**

*Additional Lyrics*

3. You know it's up to you, I think it's only fair.
   Pride can hurt you too. Apologize to her.
   Because she loves you and you know that can't be bad.
   Yes, she loves you and you know you should be glad.

# Strawberry Fields Forever

**Words and Music by John Lennon and Paul McCartney**

Copyright © 1967 Sony/ATV Music Publishing LLC
Copyright Renewed
This arrangement Copyright © 2009 Sony/ATV Music Publishing LLC
All Rights Administered by Sony/ATV Music Publishing LLC, 8 Music Square West, Nashville, TN 37203
International Copyright Secured   All Rights Reserved

*Additional Lyrics*

3. Always know, sometimes think it's me,
But you know I know when it's a dream.
I think I know, I mean, ah yes, but it's all wrong.
That is, I think I disagree.

# Ticket to Ride

**Words and Music by John Lennon and Paul McCartney**

Copyright © 1965 Sony/ATV Music Publishing LLC
Copyright Renewed
This arrangement Copyright © 2009 Sony/ATV Music Publishing LLC
All Rights Administered by Sony/ATV Music Publishing LLC, 8 Music Square West, Nashville, TN 37203
International Copyright Secured   All Rights Reserved

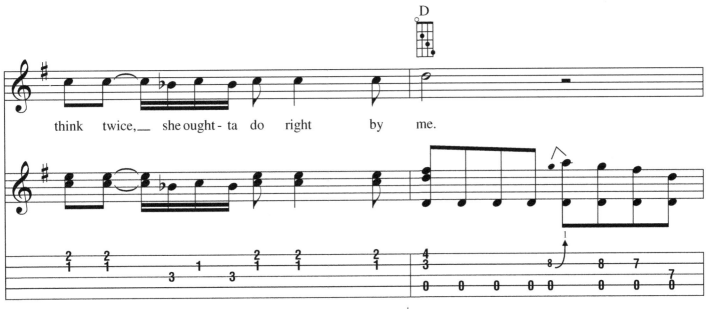

think twice,___ she ought - ta do right by me.

*D.S. al Coda*

Coda

3. I

**Outro**

G    C    G    D7    1., 2. G    3. G

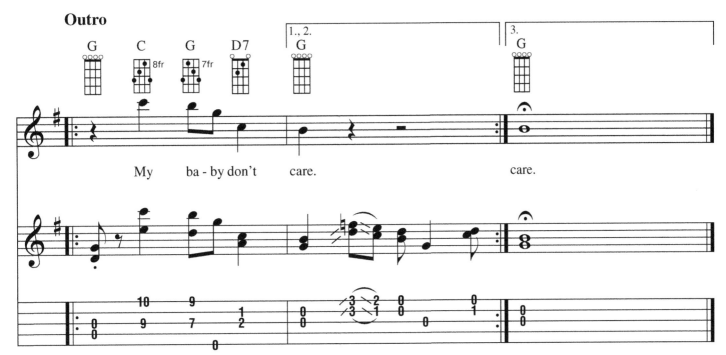

My   ba - by don't   care.      care.

# When I'm Sixty-Four

**Words and Music by John Lennon and Paul McCartney**

Copyright © 1967 Sony/ATV Music Publishing LLC
Copyright Renewed
This arrangement Copyright © 2009 Sony/ATV Music Publishing LLC
All Rights Administered by Sony/ATV Music Publishing LLC, 8 Music Square West, Nashville, TN 37203
International Copyright Secured   All Rights Reserved

**2nd time, D.S. al Coda**

*Additional Lyrics*

3. Send me a postcard, drop me a line, stating point of view.
   Indicate precisely what you mean to say.
   Yours sincerely wasting away.
   Give me your answer, fill in a form, mine forevermore.
   A-will you still need me, will you still feed me, when I'm sixty-four?

# You've Got to Hide Your Love Away

**Words and Music by John Lennon and Paul McCartney**

1. Here I stand, head in hand,— turn my face to the
2. *See additional lyrics*

wall.          If she's gone, I can't go on,— feel-ing two foot small.___

\* Arranged for basic strum or clawhammer style; index finger picks melody notes.

Copyright © 1965 Sony/ATV Music Publishing LLC
Copyright Renewed
This arrangement Copyright © 2009 Sony/ATV Music Publishing LLC
All Rights Administered by Sony/ATV Music Publishing LLC, 8 Music Square West, Nashville, TN 37203
International Copyright Secured   All Rights Reserved

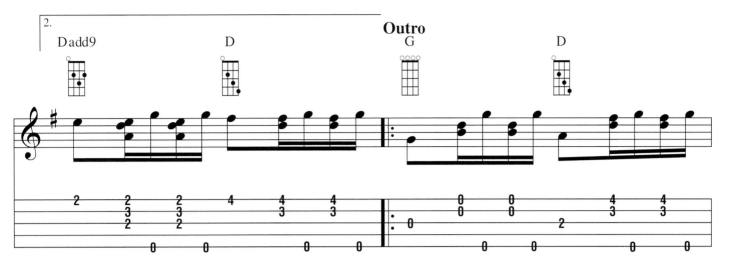

**Outro**

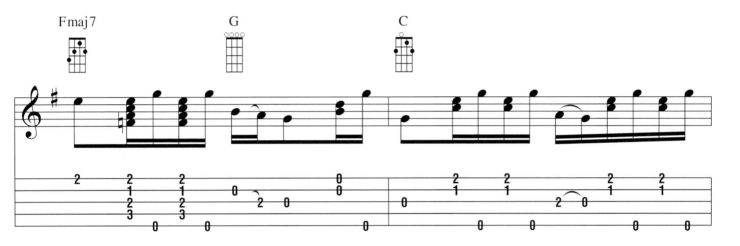

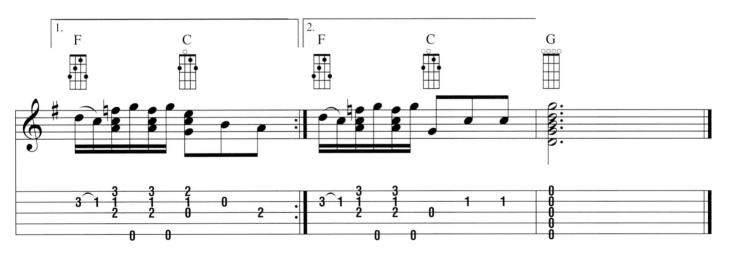

*Additional Lyrics*

2. How can I even try? I can never win,
   Hearing them, seeing them, in the state I'm in.
   How could she say to me love will find a way?
   Gather 'round all you clowns, let me hear you say:

# Yesterday

**Words and Music by John Lennon and Paul McCartney**

Copyright © 1965 Sony/ATV Music Publishing LLC
Copyright Renewed
This arrangement Copyright © 2009 Sony/ATV Music Publishing LLC
All Rights Administered by Sony/ATV Music Publishing LLC, 8 Music Square West, Nashville, TN 37203
International Copyright Secured   All Rights Reserved

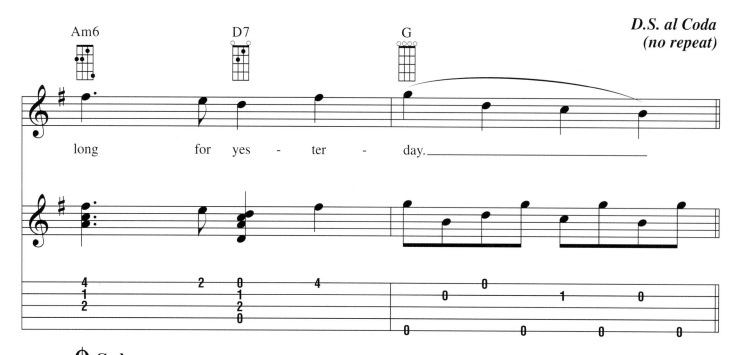

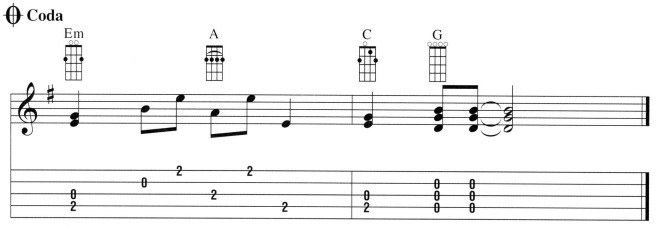

*Additional Lyrics*

3. Yesterday, love was such an easy game to play.
   Now I need a place to hide away.
   Oh, I believe in yesterday.